NO FIXED ABODE

THE FRENCH LIST

MARC AUGÉ

NO FIXED ABODE
Ethnofiction

TRANSLATED BY CHRIS TURNER

LONDON NEW YORK CALCUTTA

The work is published with the support of the
Publication Assistance Programmes of the Institut français

The publication of this volume is also
supported by the Centre national du livre (CNL),
Ministry of Culture, France.

Seagull Books, 2018

First published in French as *Journal d'un SDF: Ethnofiction*

© Editions du Seuil, Paris, 2011
Collection La Librarie du XXIe siècle, sous la direction de Maurice Olender

First published in English translation by Seagull Books, 2013

English translation © Chris Turner, 2013

ISBN   978 0 8574 2 634 5

British Library Cataloguing-in-Publication Data
A catalogue record for this book is available from the British Library.

Typeset in Dante MT by Seagull Books, Calcutta, India
Printed and bound by Hyam Enterprises, Calcutta, India

CONTENTS

TRANSLATOR'S NOTE

I would like to thank Marie-Dominique Maison for the most helpful discussions I have had with her over a number of questions arising from this text. There are no notes in the original. Those provided in this translation are my own.

Chris Turner
Birmingham, 2012

In recent years, social workers or members of charitable organizations have pointed out the appearance of a new category among the poor. The people concerned have jobs, but their income is insufficient to pay rent. They live wherever they can—in hostels, with friends or even in their cars. In some French local authorities, the public services refer to them as SDS (*Sans Domicile Stable*: of no stable abode), a term that is supposed to differentiate them from those who are genuinely 'of no fixed abode'. The phenomenon isn't a rare one. And it is spreading. Véronique Vasseur, chief medical officer at the Santé Prison, highlights it in one of her books, *A la rue* (*On the Streets*, 2008).

In the present volume I have tried to imagine how one of these new drifters gets into this position. This is neither an academic study nor a novel but an 'ethnofiction'.

What is an ethnofiction? A narrative that evokes a social fact through the subjectivity of a particular individual. However, since this is neither autobiography nor confession, that fictional individual has to be created 'from scratch' or, in other words, out of the thousand and one details observed in everyday life.

Why this recourse to fiction? In his *Introduction to the Work of Marcel Mauss*, Claude Lévi-Strauss pointed out that to grasp the notion of the 'total social fact' fully, you would have to be able to incorporate into it the subjective visions of each of those who have a part in it.[1] Here I do the opposite: I describe an individual situation and a particular subjectivity and I leave it to the readers to imagine the social totality it expresses in its way—a social totality of which they can themselves, over time, form a more or less precise idea from the Press, the news and from conversations they might have with different people.

As for the effects and the ramifications in the individual consciousness of a situation brought about by a general phenomenon that we sum up in ready-made expressions ('crisis', 'unemployment', 'household confidence') and objective statistics, these are something we have to try to imagine. And, indeed, that is what those who are 'surveyed' do, for their part, when they reply to the questionnaires designed for them. The sociologists who gather their responses transform the answers into objective data. But the selection of the items and the exploitation of the responses mask narratives that will never emerge into the light. To imagine one of these narratives is certainly of the order of fiction, as is every life-narrative, including the autobiographical one which is, primarily, a reconstruction.

---

1 Claude Lévi-Strauss, *Introduction to the Work of Marcel Mauss* (Felicity Baker trans.) (London: Routledge and Kegan Paul, 1987).

Truth is not the literal transcription (supposing such a thing were possible) of the elements of reality. Novelists know this, but they sometimes take as a starting point, before flying free of it, a theme, word or concept borrowed from anthropology. The anthropologist here is doing the opposite: he is using the novelist's mode of exposition to suggest the fleshly totality of emotion, uncertainty or anxiety concealed within the themes he has picked out, the words he has used and the concepts he has tried to develop—in this particular case, for example, those of *place* and *non-place*.

The ethnofiction author does not have the same ambition as the novelist. He does not want his readers to identify with or 'believe in' his 'protagonist' but, rather, to discover in him something of their times and in that sense—and that sense alone—to recognize themselves or see something of themselves in him. The character round which an ethnofiction is built is, in any event, a witness to his or her times and, in the best of cases, a symbol.

You have only to have moved house once or twice in your life to be able to imagine, without too much difficulty, the destructive effects wrought by the loss of spatio-temporal markers. It is no longer just psychology that is at issue in the situation of the homeless but, directly, the sense of relationship, identity and being. Voltaire's Candide or Montesquieu's Persian were characters from ethnofiction but they looked at the world and were amazed by it.[2] Today it is in looking at himself that the ethnofictional character discovers the world's madness.

Marc Augé

---

2 Voltaire, *Candide, or Optimism* (T. Cuffe trans.) (Harmondsworth: Penguin, 2005); Montesquieu, *Persian Letters* (C. J. Betts trans.) (Harmondsworth: Penguin, 1973).

Wednesday, 19 March

I've always dreamt about escaping. It's a recurrent night-time scene. The scenario's never entirely the same but each time I find myself surrounded by enemies who've miraculously failed to notice my presence. And the ending recurs in one of two ways: either I sneak off quietly, trying not to be spotted, or I succumb to panic and high tail it at top speed, as though the devil were on my heels. Sometimes I go from the one to the other in the same dream. While I'm trying to slip away discreetly, someone notices and points me out and then it's a case of headlong flight. Whatever the way of it, the outcome is always the same. I wake up suddenly, shaken and upset, and the relief at having escaped my demons—those demons I can't identify but which return regularly to haunt me—soon gives way to anxiety at having to face the tedium of the daily round.

In waking life, by contrast, as soon as I allow myself to imagine it might be possible, after all, to drop everything that's apparently so natural and yet so burdensome and take off for somewhere else, my pulse races, flushes of happiness rob me of my breath and I almost suffocate. Then everything calms down and goes back to normal again. I'm like those static opera choruses singing, 'March, march!' I'm dreaming but I'm going nowhere.

Today, I'd rather like to know whether my imminent departure from my flat will mark a beginning or an ending. It's perhaps naive to be asking oneself such a question at my age but life is no respecter of age. The duress I'm under is unexpected but inescapable. I need to find my bearings. Being forced to act for once, I'm not sure whether I'm on the eve of a new departure or a definitive collapse. I'm going to take stock, then, but I'll try to stick to the calculable aspect of things. After all, that's what's at issue.

My pension as a tax inspector amounts to a little less than two thousand euros a month. My first marriage, an age ago, ended less than four years later in divorce. That brought me a life sentence: 'spousal support', indexed to something or other, which now stands at eight hundred and fifty euros a month. None of that would be too serious if it weren't for my second, recent divorce. My wife's salary—she worked in the tax office too—more or less paid the rent and a few fixed charges. Mine paid for our food. She didn't want anything from me—you can't get blood out of a stone—but she's gone to live elsewhere, leaving me the apartment. That's fourteen hundred euros a month plus extra charges. Do the maths.

Friday, 21 March

The antique dealer has been. Well, he was more of a small-time second-hand dealer really. But he had a sharp eye and a greedy one too. I knew right away he was going to fleece me. His way of talking nineteen to the dozen wearied me from the start. The way he said 'sincerely' or 'I'm telling you straight' at every verse end soon came to seem like a recurrent mark of deceitfulness. Yet I knew immediately I was going to accept his offer without demur. I was paralyzed by a desire to be done with it all. I haggled a bit over the price of the chest of drawers, an eighteenth-century piece inherited from my mother a decade ago. I'd always been told it was authentic. 'A splendid piece,' the removal man had said when he'd hoisted it up in the apartment. 'If you'd rather, we can get an evaluation from the Drouot auction house,' the dealer suggested, 'but that'll take time.' I declined. In the end he agreed to take everything away within the week, including the old fridge and the battered cooker, and he wrote me a cheque for four thousand euros. I knew it was a way of forcing my hand, but what of it? He asked me if I could wait a few days before cashing the cheque. 'There's just enough in my account,' he explained, 'but I'm going to do a market in the provinces next Tuesday and I'll have more ready cash then.'

The toughest moment for me was when he and his two helpers—Indians or Pakistanis, I'm not sure which—cleared the bedroom. 'Might as well start right away,' he announced. 'Would you mind if I take your bed? There's nothing to be had from the bed base and the mattress, and your wardrobe isn't anything to speak of, but we'll be ahead of the game for Monday.' I said I didn't mind; I'd sleep on the living-room sofa. I told him not to forget the wall mirror (we bought it at the Saint-Ouen flea market) and to take all the little knick-knacks, the little boxes with him—and even the postcards that were cluttering up the mantelpiece. He asked my permission to take away a dress that my wife had forgotten and left behind in the wardrobe. In the twinkling of an eye I found myself in an absolutely bare room.

The advantage of this total clearout is that I'll avoid the need to pay for storage. I haven't said anything to anyone. I've nothing on my hands now and nothing up my sleeve. Better than a conjuror, it's myself I'm making disappear.

I thought I might look for a little studio flat, what the property adverts call a *studette*—just a place to sleep, a dozen square metres or so with a kitchenette and a shower corner. But, in spite of all the dinky little diminutives used by the advertisers, you can't find a broom cupboard for less than six hundred euros a month, even in the poorer north-eastern areas of the city. And then there'd still be some service charges on top. I wouldn't get far with the four or five hundred euros I'd have left. To get back to a little comfort, I absolutely have to claw back the costs of rent, landline and television. I'm going to give up on my mobile too. It's no use, except for getting calls from people who are either tiresome or don't mean very much to me. But those bastards always make you sign ridiculous contracts and I get the feeling it'll cost me plenty to get off the hook. Since it's only telephones we're talking about, I should perhaps say it'll cost me plenty to 'give it up' but with soft drugs like mobile phones or news broadcasts, 'getting off the hook' is probably the right expression after all.

I'll go and see the caretaker tomorrow. She knows I'm leaving and I'm going to ask her to get the owner of the building to come round—or, rather, the representatives of the insurance company that owns it. I've two months' deposit to get back. There's going to have to be some tough talking over the holes in the wall and the places where the ceiling's peeling away—normal wear and tear, your honour! I can already sense they'll beat me down over the deposit and I won't protest. It isn't that they frighten me but I really hate arguing with those kinds of people. The caretaker I really like. She's noticed I've been living alone for a few months now but she's been discreet about it. She confided to me the other day that she and her husband are going back to Portugal in 2013, to their village in the south, and she's scared she'll be bored there.

Perhaps she was trying to draw me into divulging my own little secret but I didn't unbend.

Monday, 24 March

The dealer and his two confederates arrived at the crack of dawn. I heard the key in the lock. I'd barely had time to get off the sofa before they were at work in the dining room and at the kitchenette. They emptied the dresser and the cupboards. I offered them a coffee. They had one with me and then the two employees rinsed out the coffee pot and the cracked bowls we'd just been using. They skilfully wrapped each cup, plate and glass in newspaper. Even the packet of coffee disappeared. 'Porcelain and crystalware are what sell best,' said the dealer with a knowing wink. He also packed off a little bronze statue that he'd had his eye on from the beginning. He'd noticed it right away on Friday and I'd spotted his interest, even though he worked hard to conceal it. He was all over it again today. He grasped it casually, half-heartedly, examined it for a few seconds with a doubtful look, weighed it in his hand, turned it all ways in a mock-playful manner— but actually to check if it was signed—then passed it on hastily to the packer, muttering 'We'll see what we can get for that.' 'We go this evening,' he added, 'and we'll be back tomorrow night. Don't worry, we'll be here on Wednesday.'

I told myself I was being too naive. For a moment, I even wondered if he'd come back, now that he had his hands on the things that were apparently worth his trouble. But I remembered the chest of drawers was still there and that reassured me.

In the evening, I went down to the garage. The old Mercedes, bought for a song last year from a wealthy colleague who wanted to get a new one, still looks good despite its eighteen years of age. I lay down on the back seat. It's a bit hard but spacious. I could almost stretch my legs right out. I went back up and rummaged round in the mountain of bedding and clothing cluttering the hallway. I pulled out a pillow and two blankets and took them down to the car. I went to buy a farmhouse-bread sandwich from the baker's, then popped to the Tunisian grocer's for a bottle of beer. This evening I'll give myself a last night in front of the television, curled up snugly on the sofa. To celebrate the event, I've even decided to finish the bottle of whisky that's been lying about in the kitchen. Just a few drops, that's all, but they put some heart into me. I'll go back down to the garage around midnight. There isn't much chance of meeting anyone at that time. There are only old people and big families in the building. I'll sleep in the car, to get myself into training.

Tuesday, 25 March

I managed to doze a bit but woke around five. It took me a few seconds to realize where I was. Perhaps I'm mildly claustrophobic: through the back window the ceiling of the underground garage seemed very low, oppressive even. I went back up to the flat. I didn't, after all, want to be caught sleeping in my car by the man from across the landing. I took a shower and started to pack. I need to be methodical if I'm to make an accurate assessment of my needs. The main thing, the number one concern, is absolutely not to look like someone who's sleeping rough. So I put my two classic suits into the first case and check that the Order of Merit ribbon is clearly visible on the buttonhole of the two jackets. On top of the suits I put three white shirts that are in good condition and two ties I never wear but which may have a role to play in the future. It's time to pay attention to external signs of respectability and think about dressing conventionally. I also set aside my only presentable pair of shoes and some socks. I put some underwear in the second case and my toothbrush and shaving gear into a little sports bag. The big issue is going to be washing and shaving. I take the two cases down to the garage and put them in the boot of the car. It's huge. They'll be easy to move and open. The boot's becoming a kind of storage unit, a sort of late twentieth-century chest of drawers. The inside of the car is the wardrobe part: I hang up an over-coat and a raincoat on the hooks provided for the purpose. Everything is ready, or almost. I feel a bit like a young boy scout about to prepare for his first camping trip.

I have use of the garage and the flat until the end of the month—enjoyment of them, as the con-tract says. That makes a few days yet. But what strange enjoyment. In the garage, whose low ceiling makes me anxious, there's a vague smell of petrol which soon becomes sickly, and tomorrow or the day after there'll be nothing left in the flat. I tot up my money, then go over it again and find that I'm almost rich. I've three thousand euros in my savings account, a bit less than a thousand in my current account and a cheque for four thousand euros in my pocket. I'm going to get at least a thousand euros of deposit back and, at the end of the month, I'll get the eleven hundred euros that are left after the support payment has been automatically deducted.

This afternoon I'll make a detailed exploration of the surrounding area. Soon my only problem will be where to park the car. Not so long ago, there were streets that still had no parking meters and, if you were patient, you could find some free spots. But that golden age has come to an end and, even round the big outer boulevards—even between those boulevards and the ring road—the parking-ticket merchants check out the tiniest side streets and remotest culs-de-sac.

Loneliness—it's best to call it by its name—has nothing unbearable about it. Silence is less annoying than the efforts aimed at overcoming it, and it's infinitely less painful to be quiet on your own than when there's two of you.

If I've decided to make these notes day by day, it's pretty much with the sense of addressing an unknown witness, who isn't really me but a sort of imaginary reader. A reader I'll feel a little closer to each today, by force of habit. I'd like to regard the course of my life as a story I could get caught up in. If that story is tellable, then there's a certain logic to it; it isn't completely mad. So I shall tell it. I decided yesterday to lay down a sort of rule for myself and work at the computer for at least an hour a day, whether or not I felt any inspiration. Soon I'll have neither tables nor chairs but there are lots of cafes in the area and my car's comfortable.

My loneliness isn't something new. What is new, and gives me a mild sense of intoxication or dizziness, is the certainty that I can do whatever I like without anyone knowing. I've no relatives any more, except a very distant cousin, and I don't even know if he's still alive. I have some colleagues I see occasionally. Those who are retired like me mostly live in the provinces. My old friend Albert, whom I knew in the sixth form at school and could talk to about anything—life, death, love and the rest—has been living deep in the Auvergne since he took early retirement three or four years ago.

Wednesday, 26 March

They came around noon. The dealer was full of the joys of spring. He apologized. 'We're a bit late but we needed to recover. It was a good sale, I'm telling you straight. You brought me luck.' He winked at me again, the same as before, and went on jabbering away in an unflaggingly good mood. 'We're really up for it now. Oh, by the way, you can pay your cheque in.' He was really keen to persuade me we'd both got a good deal.

By three o'clock they'd finished. We shook hands. He said, 'Till the next time!' It wasn't a joke—which I could, after all, have found offensive —but an all-purpose formula used unthinkingly. Mentally, he was already elsewhere. I walked round the deserted flat a little. Then, with my laptop tucked under my arm, went off to have a beer at the Rendez-vous des amis.

At the Rendez-vous des amis, they talk about anything and everything, though the precise topics of conversation depend on the time of day and the clientele. Early in the morning, a few clerical workers from an annex to the police headquarters, which is nearby, and some old single men from the neighbourhood come and have a coffee there and comment on the news, by which I mean yesterday's TV news programme and the headlines in the *Parisien*, which is provided with the landlord's compliments. In actual fact, they talk mainly about how the football league's going. One or two of the single men linger for part of the morning over a glass of wine. They philosophize or talk politics without any great passion. Noon brings the crowds: students from a neighbouring commercial college come in to join the workers from the police HQ, who are back for lunch. The Rendez-vous has a good chef and takes luncheon vouchers. The youngsters, girls and boys, talk loudly and quickly. They're constantly interrupting each other, raising their voices, as though they fear they may not make themselves heard. They tell one another jokes that only they understand—about their teachers, their fellow students or classes they've had that very morning. The police HQ workers listen indulgently to their conversations. The afternoon is quieter, but from seven or eight in the evening some new people appear. These are either solitary figures or older couples who have their set ways, as in a boarding house. The evening menu (fourteen euros, dessert and small carafe of wine included) is appealing. Some artists, who live in a block two streets further down, and even a number of tourists, who've heard about the place by word of mouth or from the *Guide du Routard*, come more occasionally. In the evening, it's not unusual to hear two or three languages spoken. Maria, the *patronne*, is Spanish and when compatriots come to taste her food she goes into top gear. She runs from table to table, shouts to everyone, sings, throws in a dance step or two and generally has a whale of a time under the placid eye of Robert, her Norman husband. Between these bursts of action, she always seems a little vacant; I suspect she's a bit of a depressive.

This afternoon we're in the slack period. Maria is leaning on the bar and leafing abstractedly through a magazine. I take a seat and ask for a beer. When she places it in front of me, she smiles wanly and mumbles, 'Dreary weather, isn't it?' I assent. Dreary weather.

It's a big first tonight. I dined at the Rendez-vous des amis, walked down as far as place de la Convention, with half a mind to go to the cinema. There was nothing really tempting on. I wandered round the neighbourhood a little, then came back up to the flat. Lying on the floor, I listened to the wireless. My transistor radio is the only piece of furniture I still possess. The French are concerned, it seems, about their purchasing power. I can understand them. I went to vote the other day—not out of a sense of conviction but to establish in my own eyes the respectability I would soon be needing so greatly, since, on the evening of the 31st, I shall be homeless. A top-of-the-range homeless person but homeless all the same. I switch off the *France Info* radio station. I'm going to go down to the garage, take the car and find a quiet place over by rue Brancion. The neighbourhood's actually a more

14

'happening' place than it seems and parking places aren't freed up until midnight or one o'clock, when the restaurants turn out.

Friday, 28 March

The night went well. Obviously, it was just a rehearsal. When I slid into the back of the car, took my shoes off and stretched out on the back seat, I had a sense of doing something wrong. I'd crossed the forbidden frontier. My parents came fleetingly into my mind, as though I still had to justify myself over a course of action which would, in their eyes, have set the seal of failure on the whole of a life. But they weren't around any more. No one was. No one was asking me to account for myself. After a few minutes' silence, I calmed down. I experienced a muted sense of joy: I'd done it!

I fell asleep. I woke up several times during the night. I stuck my head out from under the blanket. The wind had got up and the leaves of the tree I'd parked beneath were fluttering around in a strange chiaroscuro. All of this played into a sense of rural comfort—or even seaside luxury—as though I were parked a few metres from the seashore. *Suave mari magno . . .*[1] But by six o'clock I was up. I like the metallic morning light in this month of March, that particular moment when, for a few minutes, the sky, washed by the night, shines with an ephemeral

---

1 'Suave mari magno, turbantibus aequora ventis, / E terra magnum alterius spectare laborem' (It is sweet, when the winds disturb the waters of the vast sea, to witness from land the peril of other persons) (Lucretius, *De rerum natura*, 2.1).

gleam before the clouds arrive. I drove the car back to the underground car park. At seven o'clock, having showered and made myself 'clean as a new pin', as my grandmother used to say, I lingered over a black coffee in a *café-tabac* at the top of rue Brancion. I *savoured* it, drinking it down slowly, drop by drop, taking my time since the croissants, whose exceptional moistness I'd already had occasion to appreciate once or twice, never arrived before 7.30.

I've been recce-ing for two days now to see how to park my car for free without picking up a ticket. A seemingly impossible challenge for an ordinary mortal but I have a few cards up my sleeve. I'm familiar with the terrain and have all the time in the world to monitor the enemy's movements. The battleground is easy to define. The parc Georges-Brassens on the site of the old Vaugirard slaughterhouses is bordered, at its base, by the rue des Morillons and, when you look towards the outer boulevards, by the rue de Dantzig on its right and the rue de Brancion on its left. It's generally around ten or eleven in the morning that a police van drops off a squad of *flics* of both sexes at the top of the rue de Dantzig. They move slowly down the street, slapping tickets on the guilty cars. They sometimes come back that way in the afternoon but never after half past four. In the morning, they also operate in the rue des Morillons. By contrast, it's in the middle of the afternoon, never before three o'clock and most often around four or five, that another squad are let loose in the area around rue Brancion. As a result, an attentive observer, provided he has a little time on his hands, which is clearly the case with me, can move his vehicle about in response to these more or less regular schedules and escape the vigilance of the forces of law and order by taking over at the appropriate times the places freed up by the law-abiding citizenry. And, while doing so, he can enjoy the landscape to his heart's content.

The parc Brassens was designed with great skill and seems larger than it actually is. A wall of council blocks separates it from the outer boulevard the way a cliff separates the land from the sea. Seen from a distance, particularly at night, the blocks don't look too bad. By night, their massive architecture, studded with many lights, adds to the surrealist character of the site, which strikes you forcibly when, at the entrance to the park, you come across not only two great bovine statues, which make a sort of strange war monument, but two quaint, gaunt houses with red tile roofs which, under the street lights, seem to have come straight out of a painting by Paul Delvaux.[2] Since I don't intend to leave a forwarding address with the caretaker, I could perhaps spare myself all these calculations. But it would be dangerous, after all, to pile up a series of fines. I've gone over to the other side now

---

2 Paul Delvaux (1897–1994) was a Belgian painter connected with the surrealist movement.

and the enemy might lay an ambush for me, particularly as I'm going to be noticed in the neighbourhood with my Mercedes.

The fact is, I don't want to take the plunge right away. I'm not in a hurry for a change of scenery. I'm planning on staying around here for a while, without telling anyone anything about my situation. I'm used to things here and know the local shopkeepers. But none of them knows exactly where I live. If I avoid the caretaker, perhaps I'll manage to convince myself I'm still really living in the fifteenth arrondissement, unless I go back to my original district—if I can put it that way—the fifth, not that I know anyone there any more. Or unless I set off in search of adventure, which is more or less my intention, my secret desire, the temptation that scares me a little but keeps nagging away at me all the same. I've plenty of time ahead of me, I'll wait until the nights aren't so cold.

Sunday, 30 March

It's Easter, but I won't be going hunting for eggs in the parc Brassens.

The world of my everyday life divides, like Proust's, into two 'ways': the Brancion way and the Dantzig way. On the Brancion way, the upper part of the street runs alongside the late, unlamented horse market. I once read a novel by Patrick Modiano in which he wrote of the sound of the horses' hooves as they were being led to the Vaugirard abattoirs. But those old ghosts have vanished once and for all. The market hall is home now at the weekend to an antique and second-hand book market. Heading the Dantzig way, you go past the outlying buildings from police HQ, where you find, among other things, the well-known department known as the 'lost-property' or 'lost-and-found' office, depending on whether you're a pessimist or an optimist. The two ways each have their charm and their mysteries. On the Dantzig way, up at the top of the street, there's a cul-de-sac with a number of cosy little dwellings and, behind a big metal gate, la Ruche (the Hive), an old complex of painters' studios with a prestigious history, where tomorrow's masterpieces are perhaps currently taking shape. On the Brancion way, once you've gone past the old horse market and the entrance to the Théâtre Sylvia-Montfort, concealed by the foliage of the parc Brassens, you come to a bridge that spans the old railway line known as the *petite ceinture*. I like to lean on the parapet and look down on this buried landscape that looks as though it's hollowed out its bed like a river. The rails are still there and run off into the darkness of improbable tunnels. Dense vegetation grows along the walls and, here and there, some tall trees bend towards the tracks, as if to suggest the shape of another tunnel. We're now really in the no-man's-land part of the threefold boundary represented by the *petite ceinture*, the big outer boulevards and the ring road. Of the three, the *petite ceinture*—which seems deserted but where, you sense, a number of wild animals and discreet adventurers must find refuge—does most to fuel the imagination. The three of them together make this uncertain zone the symbol of my present situation: I'm parked on the outskirts of Paris, not a stone's throw from the railway lines (and here I'm referring to the fully operational ones) that shoot out from the gare Montparnasse towards the West; I'm 'parked up', apparently waiting to depart, but where am I bound?

Once you're across the bridge, there are two hotels that aren't too dear. The first is part of a well-known chain of the one- or two-star level (seventy-seven euros a night for a single room). The other, which seems not unpleasant from the outside and clearly has some of its rooms looking out over the *petite ceinture*, attracts me initially by the reasonableness of its prices: thirty-five euros per night or forty-seven for a room with en suite facilities. I'm going to need the use of a proper bed and a shower once or twice a week. For purposes of hygiene, the railway stations are useful. The showers at the gare d'Austerlitz are very decent. I'll have to go and try out the ones at the gare Montparnasse and those at the municipal swimming baths which are just by the ring road.

I spent last night in a quiet side street. I sleep in a track suit and, so long as I still have the flat, I've no problem changing. This morning I even indulged in a little jog round the park before going up to the flat to get the clothes I'd left there. From next week on, this changing-room question is going to get tricky. Where am I going to dress? Perhaps this is only apparently a problem, after all, since before six o'clock there's no one in these quiet streets and I could walk round in the nude without offending anyone's sense of decency. The early morning light always gives me a buzz. Today, as night and winter both draw to a close, all you can hear is birdsong.

Thursday, 3 April

It's all a lot harder than I thought. Or, rather, the difficulties are different from what I had expected. No doubt that's why, these last three days, I haven't felt up to keeping my word and recording my impressions on a daily basis—'keeping my diary', as the expression goes. I've let it slip and it's only with great difficulty that I'm picking it up again this evening. In fact, I'm picking myself up. I've slipped too, like my diary, and I now have to try to pick up the pieces. A truly great result after three days of a new life! All my fine resolutions have gone west too, though admittedly the endless downpours don't make matters any easier.

On Monday I said goodbye to the caretaker. I handed back the keys and, in confidence, left her the address of my friend in the Auvergne, so that she could forward any message she sensed was urgent. To tell the truth, I immediately regretted that act of weakness, since I don't see what could be so urgent. Doubtless, without actually admitting this to myself, I wanted to feel that I wasn't severing all links with the outside world or, to be more precise—and more honest—with the past. Where the rest was concerned, I added, she should keep the few letters I might receive. My pretext here was that I was taking a long trip abroad before settling down again. I must have seemed a bit confused and

I'm not sure she believed me, but I know I can count on her.

The difficulty—and I had some prior sense of this, but it welled up all of a sudden with overwhelming, heart-rending force—was the sense of absolute loneliness. Try as I might to talk myself round, to remind myself of everything I'd said to all and sundry about the real pleasure I found in feeling alone, I had to face the fact that a rush of panic ran through me on Monday evening when I realized I no longer had anywhere to call home; that I'd cut myself adrift and couldn't talk to anyone about it; that I was drifting randomly, tossed by unknown currents, between the second-hand books and the lost property. The loss of place is like the loss of another person, of the last other person, of the ghost who welcomes you back when you come home alone.

On Tuesday and Wednesday I behaved erratically. On Tuesday I dashed off to the place Saint-Sulpice to see my former colleagues. I asked two of them out to lunch, two people I didn't know very well but who were free. From a call box, I called Albert in the Auvergne to tell him I'd like to come and see him shortly. He asked what had happened to my telephone; he'd been trying to contact me for two days. I improvised an answer: They'd been doing some work on the building, I said, and the phone was out of order. As for the mobile, I'd packed it in. 'You did right,' he replied. 'Those things are the work of the devil. All the same, give me a call to let me know when you're coming.' I went back to the place Saint-Sulpice in search of a dinner companion but everyone had gone. I caught the 89 on the rue de Rennes and took refuge in the Rendez-vous des amis where, fortunately, a group of revellers was celebrating something or other round a rather tipsy guitarist. I joined the party. Later that night, I got back to the Mercedes to find it sporting a ticket and covered in pigeon droppings. I'd drunk too much, but I slept.

On Wednesday, I stopped to talk to the hard-faced beggar who's set up a sort of little encampment at the top end of the rue de Dantzig. I've gone past there every day for at least two or three years without stopping—trying, in fact, to avoid his smell and his eyes. I engaged him in conversation and was surprised by the gentleness of his voice. He told me that a number of people in the neighbourhood helped him and that's why he stayed round. There were even people who called him by his name. I felt obliged to ask him what that name was. 'François,' he replied, 'a good, Christian name. We Christians ought to help one another.' I didn't dare ask how he went about taking a shit, which is the big problem after all, even if the Decaux company, suppliers of public conveniences, now open up their facilities free of charge, doubtless at the urging of some enlightened politicians. I think I've spotted François occasionally slipping into the sacristy of a church which is hidden away in the little courtyard that's shared by two blocks on the street. Fortunately, I haven't got to that point yet. I've already imagined, with some wry amusement, the day when, swallowing my pride and a good deal of my anti-clerical sentiment, I go and ask the parish priest for permission to use his toilet.

Saturday, 5 April

I'm clinging to the radio and my diary at the moment. Politicians do a lot of talking but it's only what they don't say that counts. Today we're being offered austerity but they don't actually use the word. The flip side of political cant is the emergence of forbidden words. 'Austerity plan,' say the one side; 'Making economies,' say the others. You'd think it was a vocabulary contest. For me, there'll be austerity and economies.

The spring that seemed to be smiling yesterday has shrouded itself in grey this morning. Grey is the colour of the news too. A Malian with no identity papers has died after jumping into the river Marne to escape an identity check.

The feeling that you have to get away from it all is stronger on some days than others. But the earth is so small and the globe so round that it's very difficult to imagine where such flight might lead.

This evening I'll sleep at the hotel—the more modest of the two, thirty-five francs—as a way of bolstering my flagging morale.

Sunday, 6 April

I listen to the radio in the half-light that comes fil-
tering through the shutters of the bedroom where
I'm having a lie-in before I go for a wash. If anyone
had told me just a few months ago that I'd one day
regard it as a luxury to share a shower and toilets
with my neighbours on the same floor . . . With
barely a hint of compassion, a calm, resonant voice
declares that it's going to rain in Paris and that it will
be cold. I really didn't need the weather forecast getting me down as well, gloomy as I've been in recent
days. I open the window. The sky is clear and the
atmosphere seemingly spring-like. Even if it surely
won't last, it's good to enjoy it while it does. I curse
the radio announcer who's spoilt this morning for
me by forecasting a downpour at the end of it. The
unbearable power of words.

And, staying with the impact of words, it seems
a government minister, who yesterday in an inter-
view with *Le Monde* laid down the 'conditions' on
which the French president would agree to go to
Beijing for the opening of the Olympic Games, had
by the evening to deny she had used those words.
There's endless debate this morning over the meaning of the word 'condition'. The surrealist side of
politics has become more tangible each day since I
became homeless. Current events are recounted to
us like a soap opera. Our attention is brought to
bear on questions that are formulated for us, but as

though we'd raised them ourselves: questions we end up repeating as though we ourselves thought them up. Will the 'humanitarian unit' leave Colombia? Will the Olympic torch get across Paris without incident? Has contact been made with the Somali pirates? These questions focus attention on certain facts while at the same time reducing them to the particular episodes they relate to at that time. Having said that, on this special holiday, when I'm enjoying the luxury of a proper bed, I wallow voluptuously in current affairs and I look forward almost with pleasure to the evening that's to come, listening to *France Info* in the cosy darkness of my Mercedes. I should say that I bought a sleeping bag yesterday.

Tuesday, 8 April

One of those days when, if you judge by the news, nothing is happening. I throw myself into Kafka's *Diaries*, which has just been republished with other fragments and I come upon this passage in his 'Meditations':

> 'You keep talking about death and yet you do not die,'

> And yet I shall die. What I am writing is my swansong. One man's song is longer, another man's song is shorter. But the difference is only ever a matter of a few words.

> Taking writing seriously, taking it 'at its word' —doesn't that mean writing as though you were to die the minute you stopped?

> But what am I talking about? Who do I take myself for? I prefer not to answer, so as not to give in to despondency.

Thursday, 10 April

In *Libération*, which I leaf through this morning as I have my coffee and a croissant in the *bar-tabac* at the top end of the rue Brancion, an article on an inside page grabs my attention. It points out that energy in France is becoming a source of added inequality. The proportion of expenditure on energy in French household budgets varies depending on people's place of residence and their income. It has fallen for the richest households and risen to ten or fifteen per cent for the poorest. The gap is growing, then, between the two extremes of the social spectrum.

All things considered, I'm not doing too badly.

Monday, 14 April

After a few days of drifting, I get a grip on myself again. I settle down, accustom myself to the change and get myself organized. But I should really make an even greater break with the past, to use a phrase dear to our politicians. This diary, to begin with. I've given up writing it every day. Sometimes I've nothing to talk about except my tiredness. Then the diary isn't the piece of writing I cling to in order to help me through the day, but a mere pretext, an experience of emptiness and aridity, like the topical events I pretend to comment on. Just as I've given up my mobile and TV, I'm going to give up plagiarism, give up plagiarizing the trivia they shower on us every day of the week. I'll take it all in and swallow it down like the others, somewhat shamefacedly, though not without a certain pleasure at times. But I shan't pay it the compliment of adding my own comments. My morning press review is finished. I'm closing it down. Sarkozy, Putin, Bush and the others can go hang. I'll have nothing to do with them—at least, I'll write nothing about them. On the other hand, I'm very much aware that every three or four days, like today, I feel a real need not to lose sight of myself—to take stock and go back over states of mind, the content and meaning of which escaped me at the time. Instead of reporting things 'live', then, I'm going to do it with a slight delay, like Chinese TV at the Beijing Olympics. In the meantime, I might, if I really fancy it, write something else. An idea for a short story's been going round in my head for some days now. I spent a few hours in the calm solitude of the Rendez-vous this afternoon thinking about it and even trying to write it. That reminded me of those lazy, tortured months long ago when I gave up my academic ambitions for a writing career and then, when my first manuscript was rejected, gave up the writing career and became a tax inspector. The sudden desire I feel today to turn my personal story completely around—to live it in reverse and go back to writing now that the tax department has pensioned me off—comes from a vengeful obstinacy that, at my age, has perhaps something pathological about it. But it helps me bear the discomfort of daily life.

Thanks to the implementation of the slight delay, I can already better gauge the significance of the quiet revolution I've just carried through. Not only, as I hoped, has nothing changed in my relations with the shopkeepers, but those relations have —how can I put it?—intensified. When I go into a shop, it's plain I'm in less of a hurry than before. I'm more attentive and chattier. And the people I speak to there respond to my charm offensive straight away. We're now visibly chummy. It has to be said, too, that I'm always neatly turned out and my tie and the little blue ribbon in my buttonhole make a good impression. With the butcher—from whom I often buy ready meals that need to be re-heated in the microwave—the weather, the traffic and, with rather more caution, politics have now become the subject of the daily exchanges, eloquent insinuations and sarcastic sighs that precede the concluding 'Have a good day!' which sets the seal on our new-found closeness. I go from the butcher's to the baker's. For years, after I'd chosen either a whole-grain loaf—because the 'grains' in question have a pleasant crunch to them—or a sliced wholemeal—because it doesn't make so many crumbs in the car—she would invariably ask, 'Anything else?' in a listless, world-weary way. Now, instead of replying 'No, that's all, thanks,' I simply linger while my eyes rove over the chocolate éclairs, coffee *religieuses* and lemon tarts. I hesitate, she makes a suggestion and I go along with it. For some days now, she's been getting in first: as soon as she sees me, she recommends her vanilla slices that are 'just out of the oven' or her first strawberry tarts. Our harmonious understanding rests, then, on a narrowly technical basis but it's already beginning to extend to meteorology. I also get a *Bonjour, monsieur . . .* right away which, though it fades off into a sort of rumbling noise because she doesn't know my name, stamps me as a recognized, familiar customer. The dry-cleaner's plays a central role in my scheme, of course, and I'm treated as a friend of the establishment. I'm a homeless person but a clean-cut one. If I add in the fact that I'm at the Rendez-vous des amis every day and the *bar-tabac* at the top of the rue Brancion, then I can say I've made my niche in the area or, to be more precise, that I've nestled into it with renewed determination.

Parisians are like birds in the countryside. The year we spent our holidays in a rented cottage in Normandy, I noticed that the birds that were regular visitors to the garden—the robins, tits or blackbirds—acted as if confined to a virtual cage: they never went beyond a very restricted area and you very soon came to recognize them. In Paris, at least in the fifteenth arrondissement, it's the same with humans. We talk about the area of town we live in but that area is itself divided into little sectors, usually centred on a bakery. It's that little sector I stick to—marked out also by the butcher's, the Tunisian grocer's and a cafe-restaurant—because it confers a kind of territorial identity on me. To go two or three hundred yards down the road is to be somewhere else—a different baker's, different butcher's, different grocer's—except where some shops are concerned, such as the chemist's, the dry cleaner's or the little supermarket, which have a slightly wider range.

April (the 28th)

Yesterday afternoon, after I'd taken refuge with my computer at the Rendez-vous des amis to see if I could manage to write a few lines, a young woman came up to me and, speaking as though we knew each other, asked in a vaguely chummy way, 'How are you today?' I looked at her in some surprise. It seemed to me I knew her from somewhere. She wasn't as young as all that, in fact—perhaps forty or forty-five—but her clothes (wide khaki cotton trousers, pink blouse with a few splodges of paint on it, hairslide stuck in crossways to hold in place a plentiful head of auburn hair with a few grey streaks) and clear, bright eyes lent her quite a pleasant, youthful—or, rather, ageless—appearance. Sensing my hesitation, she came to my aid and introduced herself: 'I'm Dominique. We had dinner together the other evening, with Jacques the guitarist and all the gang. But we were at opposite ends of the table . . .' I apologized, without knowing precisely whether I was apologizing for not having recognized her immediately or for butting in among her group of friends. 'I forced myself on you a bit . . .' She burst out laughing. 'No one forces themselves on that bunch,' she assured me. When they're on form they draw in all comers. They don't like to drink alone and yet they know one another too well. They need an audience and a fresh stimulus.' I'd come along, she said, at just the right moment.

We chatted. She spoke more than I did. If I've understood her rightly, she makes composite artworks, part painted, part photographic, semi-abstract, semi-figurative compositions. In them she represents all the impersonal but familiar spaces we frequent nowadays: motorways, supermarkets, railway stations, airports . . . Her slightly muted voice isn't without its charm and I enjoyed listening to her. There were moments when she seemed amazingly young.

May

I'm getting used to my new life at last. Being without my mobile and the television gives me a sense of freedom. No one can catch up with me and my escape is going nicely, without any sort of hindrance. I've begun to make long trips around Paris, mostly on foot. When I head back towards the fifteenth arrondissement, the pleasure I get from discovering places or views I didn't previously know is added to now by the pleasure of returning, with the accompanying illusion that I really am coming home. In the back of the Mercedes, I've installed side by side my transistor radio, a big electric torch, my toilet bag, a bottle of water that I replace each day, and a bottle of whisky that I'm making last—a little swig each evening helps me to dispel the anxiety that rears its head from time to time. When I decide to turn in for the night and stretch out on the back seat, this little kit is all there by my head, ready for use. I turn on the radio and I'm home.

I generally make my big trips round Paris on foot. Sometimes I resort to the bus or the Métro, shuttles taking me into orbit. These trips are helping me rediscover the city. They bring a change of scenery, taking me out of the three areas familiar to me—the one where I lived for some years, the one I was lucky enough to work in for a long time and the one where I spent my childhood. I launch myself off into less well-known parts of the city for the pleasure of the few seconds when, as I exit the Métro, I don't know where I am. That impression doesn't last, because, as a Parisian of long standing, I quite quickly recover my bearings, but it's a dizzying one nonetheless. Climbing the stairs of a Métro station chosen solely for its name—because that name meant nothing to me—I emerge gradually on to the surface of the city, into a street or crossroads that initially seems unknown, and it's like a new birth. My particular situation increases the strangeness of the moment. I, who am no longer anyone, doubtless feel more intensely than more settled people—people better ensconced in life— the absolute gratuitousness of my presence in the city. I was going to say 'my presence on earth,' but that would be too metaphysical . . . In the fifteenth arrondissement—my little place in the *quinzième*— it's different. I'm establishing habits and trivial but essential social ties. Free of all nostalgia, I'm inventing characters and situations for the present moment that help me mark out the terrain of my daily life. It's as though I'm at the theatre but simultaneously as actor and audience. In the areas I'm not so familiar with, the isolation foisted on me—or which I've foisted on myself—is both more tangible and less of a problem. I'm just a stranger like any other, a sort of tourist visiting the capital. No longer having a role to play, no longer having to repress the somewhat over-invasive images of a near or distant past brings me a moment's rest.

The only drawback is having a poorer knowl-
edge of the geography and the local resources. The
fact is, I always have a toothbrush, a tube of tooth-
paste and a bar of soap in my pocket. I take advantage of the slightest opportunity to avail myself of
a bathroom. In the sixth arrondissement I know
what air to adopt in cafes like Le Rostand, Le Select
or La Coupole when I want to use the toilet facilities
without buying a drink. The trick is to show no hesitation. I act like a patron who has come in from the
terrace to satisfy a pressing need. The tie and deco-
ration help me to play my role convincingly. In the
sixth arrondissement there are, in fact, some very
convenient institutions. You can breeze right in and
the toilets couldn't be handier. The Education Ministry's a better bet than the Finance Ministry in that
regard. And the Maison des sciences de l'homme in
the boulevard Raspail, for example, is a far more
accessible haven than the Tax Office on the place
Saint-Sulpice. If I turned up at place Saint-Sulpice
every day, they'd begin to worry. However, with uni-
versity establishments it's just the opposite. You've
only to maintain a regular presence to pass unno-
ticed. At the Maison des sciences de l'homme
there's a cafeteria where you can get sandwiches
quite cheaply. I go at least once or twice a week.
They recognize me now and one of the staff knows
I like my coffee strong. Sometimes I go through the
Jardin du Luxembourg and walk up rue Soufflot.
That brings me near to the area where I lived as a

child, but I stop when I get to the *mairie* of the fifth arrondissement. I once swore, with two of my sixth-form friends, that I'd spend a night at the Hôtel des grands hommes where André Breton once lived but the opportunity never arose and these days I'm happy just to use the town hall's sanitary facilities, which are far more luxurious and better maintained than those of the universities.[3] In short, there's a whole area of Paris where I feel in my element and where I'm happy to hunker down again after my bold incursions on to the Right Bank. I sometimes tell myself that, with a little more audacity and application, I could live as a genuine parasite but, in reality, that's neither an ideal nor a necessity. Since I stopped paying rent, I've been quite comfortably off. It has to be said that a good upbringing taught me to moderate my needs and desires.

---

[3] The Hôtel des grands hommes figures in André Breton's surrealist work *Nadja* (1928), in which it is stated that he lived there around 1918.

May

I had a chat with François this morning. He's doing what I'm doing: writing. He's got himself a new notebook and is tracing words across its pages in blue biro. I slipped him a twenty-euro note and asked him what he was writing. 'I don't know,' he replied, a little nervously, hugging to his body the little fluffy toy dog he almost always has with him. I tried to ease his mind by telling him that it wasn't important, that I was writing too without knowing exactly what, and then I gave a silly laugh. He looked at me and smiled. It was surprising. I'd never seen him smile before. He said 'Goodbye' without taking his eyes off me and went on smiling. He was indicating it was time for me to go but doing so with kindness.

I'm spending hours at the Rendez-vous des amis. Maria, who's very capable with computers and likes to browse websites, though I don't know which ones, has set up a sort of little office for me at the back of the cafe and lets me use her Internet subscription. She's the brains behind the business. Her husband Robert goes to the Rungis wholesale market three times a week and serves as head waiter—and cook, too, when the African chef is away. She looks after the accounts.

So now I'm connected to the rest of the world. I surf the Web.

And then I write my diary in a half-hearted sort of way. I've explained to the *patronne* that I definitely find it easier to work in the cafe than at home. She seemed flattered by that. Every hour she brings me a beer. I'm pretty sure she only charges me for half of them. By around 7 p.m. I'm a bit drunk and ravenously hungry. Sometimes, Dominique comes by and settles into a corner with her sketchbook. She draws in silence, showing nothing to anyone— I mean neither to Maria nor me—then gets up all of a sudden and leaves, her sketchbook under her arm, tossing a casual 'Bye!' in our direction.

We were both engrossed in our respective occupations yesterday, but once or twice we exchanged a smile. On her way out, she came over to my table and planted a big kiss on my cheek, asking, 'Is your work going OK?' I replied that I really liked her and greatly appreciated our moments of silent intimacy in the bistro. The words had come to me unpremeditated. I was almost surprised to hear myself speak them but, as soon as I had, I knew they expressed my feelings exactly. She put her hand on my shoulder. 'I'll show you what I do one of these days . . . See you soon!' 'See you,' replied Maria, who was bringing me my latest beer.

May

I bumped into Duponchel as I was walking aim-lessly on the boulevard Saint-Michel. He rushed over, clearly happy to see me. He told me very kindly that the office seemed empty without me, that I was one hell of a live wire and that he missed me. I'm not really sure why—a kind of hyper-emotionality due to tiredness perhaps—but I was very touched by his words. The idea that I might be regarded as a live wire surprised me, even if I thought I could remember the—in fact, one-off—episode that could have gained me that reputation. It even moved me, though it delighted and flattered me more, since I would never have imagined any-one could miss me. I immediately accepted his offer to go home and have dinner with him there and then, taking pot luck, as it were. He called his wife, who simply asked him to pop by the baker's on his way home. We jumped onto a Number 38. They live out towards the porte d'Orléans area, in a brick building like the one I used to live in. He picked up his *baguette* and I bought a strawberry tart. His wife, whom I'd already met once or twice, welcomed me with a broad smile: 'Henri . . . I've been telling Georges for ages that we ought to get in touch. How are you?' I didn't remember us being such close friends before but it made me feel good.

A strange evening. Unable to get to sleep in the car, I mulled it over all night and I'm trying to sum it up this morning, sitting with my computer at a table outside the Rendez-vous. For two or three hours I felt I both was and wasn't the person being spoken to. Not just because I was acting a part— that happens to each of us every day and has, in fact, been my favourite pastime for quite a while—but because, at the very moment I was spouting my lies about my move, my future plans and my upcoming holidays with my family, I was telling myself I was nothing other than that part. I was lying: so much was certain. But behind my lies there was nothing. For his part, Duponchel had gone off on his favourite tack, exaggeratedly relating some of our best moments in the place Saint-Sulpice office. He'd composed the heroic saga of Duponchel and Cariou, tax inspectors. He brought up the time when a singing star came to protest against the back taxes she'd been assessed for and I treated her with merciless irony. He mentioned our boozy lunches in the bistro opposite the office and even recited the derisive poem we'd written together and given, on the day he retired, to Rossignol, the chief tax inspector, who took himself a bit too seriously, but had apparently appreciated our masterpiece without grasping all the allusions. Our career highlights, so to speak. And Madame Duponchel —Christine—smiled indulgently, listening to us playing the naughty boys. Soon, in less than three years' time, they were going to 'move down'—that was their expression—to Burgundy, her native region. They described at great length the fine red-roofed house, 'flanked by a sort of tower, like a manor house,' which she'd inherited from her parents. Duponchel smiled faintly as this imminent dream was conjured up. 'You'll come and see us, Henri,' said Christine. 'Certainly,' I replied.

And, indeed, why not? But the certainty had gone on growing within me the whole evening that I was happy not to be in their shoes, happy to have nothing in common with them, even if I liked them and indisputably found it comforting to have dinner in their company. Perhaps, ultimately, their lives were too similar to the life I'd led for many years not to make me feel slightly—very slightly—sick. At any rate, we wouldn't be having the same future. As I left their home and then all the way down the rue Alésia, which I skipped along briskly to dispel the headache brought on by too strong a Côtes du Rhone, I felt deeply happy to be going home to my old jalopy in the *quinzième*.

June

Last night I was awakened by a violent storm, just as I'd barely dropped off to sleep. I'd lowered the left rear window slightly to get a little air. The drops of rain coming in through there were beginning to tickle my nostrils. I wound the window back up completely but the heat prevented me from getting back to sleep. The rain came down much more heavily. As I was beginning to doze off, there was a knock at the door. I recognized François, who had pressed his face against the car window and was staring at me. Under the street light and in the driving rain, there was a haunted look in his eyes. The idea of offering to let him in to get some shelter crossed my mind but I rejected it immediately. I turned my head away and closed my eyes. When I opened them again, he'd disappeared. I told myself I'd give him a few euros the next morning. Then, thinking about it, I realized that what gave me an uneasy feeling wasn't so much the sight of the tramp lost in the rain as the sense of having been bearded in my lair and recognized by him.

June

I wandered slowly round the neighbourhood this afternoon. I was there, to begin with, to move the car, which was badly parked. Then I took some pleasure in it, as though I were taking stock of the features of the landscape in which I'd lived for several years, but seeing them now with a fresh eye. My perception of the area has, in fact, changed since I've been living on the street. Playing a role has brought me closer to the various shopkeepers, insofar as I try not to stand out, try to say the things they expect to hear, to repeat the standard formulas, the mundane, common-sense clichés, to act as though I really were one of those who exchange a few bits of news and a few smiles with them each day, as though, all in all, I was 'one of them'. I can allow myself this now that I'm sure I'm really not 'one of them', whereas up to my move it was, in fact, the opposite. My apparent aloofness—more a product of boredom than contempt, to be honest—was just to persuade myself that I wasn't 'one of them', when in fact I was, and even profoundly so—watching the same TV programmes, listening to the same news, and living as mechanically as the people I happened to bump into. Today, at least, I'm the only one sleeping in the street, the only one not paying property taxes. And they don't know, except for François, but François isn't one of those ordinary people you speak to.

When I say my perception of the area has changed, it isn't actually the shopkeepers I'm mainly thinking of. I'm thinking of lots of things. The architecture, for example. I've learned to look at the buildings and I find neglected elements of beauty in the most ordinary of them. The architecture of the fifties and sixties has wrought havoc round here, but lots of thirties' buildings have an elegance to them and, if you look hard, you still find little houses, English-style cottages, surprising villas and secret gardens. I'd seen all those things a long time ago, glimpsed them, had a fleeting awareness of them. Now I linger over the buildings and find pleasure in them. I live in an attractive area, I really do.

By dint of being in the street, I've also spotted some picturesque characters, some local personalities. First, there's a tall chap with pepper-and-salt hair tied back in a pony-tail who, strangely, seems always both to have time on his hands and to be busy. I sometimes see him striding down the rue des Morillons, as though he were dashing to some meeting of the utmost importance, then find him a little later by the parc Brassens, sitting at a table outside the cafe with his pals. But there are others. A handsome old man, to whom the dated term *spiv* might well be applied. Part pimp, part hoodlum. He may, poor chap, perhaps be the most innocent of men but, with his tight-fitting singlets, his white, slicked-back hair and his constantly, consciously impish or impudent eyes—despite the wrinkles that give away his age—he's irresistibly comical. I think I've noticed him taking the Number 89 almost every morning and coming back at around six in the evening. The hours he keeps, then, are as respectable as can be, but I like to imagine he goes off to keep an eye on the girls who work for him in some distant part of the city before coming home to drink an aperitif with the ladies of the neighbourhood and their husbands in the *bar-tabac* at the top of the rue Brancion and—who knows?—leaving again at night for Paris' seedier districts.

I call the first man Fernandel since his teeth resemble those of the famous comic actor, and the second 'the Spiv' for all the reasons mentioned above. Fernandel and the Spiv are simply the most conspicuous samples of a very special micro-society. In the upper storeys of the buildings, where the lower and the middling middle-class live, there are many who venture out only rarely and don't frequent the cafes. In the block I lived in for more than ten years, I didn't know anyone, even though we sometimes exchanged vague gestures of greeting between neighbours. But down at street level, at the park and in the bistros, it's different. There's movement, shouting, laughter, people getting together. I don't really know who makes up that little world. There are the caretakers from the buildings, generally Portuguese, but *they* have their own social network. There are the Arab shopkeepers. They're very sociable. They listen to the bored old ladies and strike up contact with other shopkeepers. There are also the suburbanites. Some cafe-owners and restaurateurs round here live in the suburbs. They have to get up early to open on time. Robert and Maria, for example, often talk feelingly of their fruit trees, their lawn and their lawnmower. Many of the others are young and have a host of friends who come and see them often. There are always lots of cars and motorbikes parked along the street that have out-of-town number plates. Last, there are the lonely old single people, widows and widowers who are assiduous cafe-goers and customers for the shops, in their search of someone to talk to, be it a waiter or waitress, the butcher, the grocer or the woman in the bakery—or even the supermarket check-out girl. But as regards the neighbourhood's eccentrics—Fernandel's gang or the Spiv's—I'm not so sure where they come from. Not from far away at all, that's certain. And, in fact, everyone knows them and they know everyone. Among all these different groups, they serve as go-betweens. They talk to anyone and everyone. A happy disposition is their weapon. They're the street-level stars, the pavement celebrities. Yesterday, as I was waiting my turn at the baker's, Fernandel came in and shook my hand. It felt like I'd 'arrived' socially.

By leaving my flat, I've joined the motley crew who live only at ground level—or give that impression. I can't imagine them on the upper floors. The neighbourhood's very different when you only view it from the pavement. People on the upper floors stay at home and come out only to go to work some distance away. For them, the pavement's just an area of transit to the Métro or the bus, the baker's or the supermarket. They don't linger there. They know nothing of the anxious, gossipy little crowd, a large part of whose day unfolds between the *bar-tabac* where they buy lottery tickets or back horses, the shops where they spend little and talk a lot, the park where they take little walks occasionally, eyeing the mothers and the West Indian nannies, and the barstools from which they comment on current events.

It's this street-level world I've been taking stock of this afternoon at the wheel of my car, with a sense of having acquired some brand-new memories.

July

I wake up this morning feeling stiff. When I say 'wake up', that's pushing it a bit. In fact, I spent the night somewhere between drowsing and waking fitfully. I even went out to walk about a little. I wandered round the neighbourhood between 3 and 4 a.m. At that sort of time you pass hurried figures here and there. Where they're going to or coming from you couldn't say. Last night, it was a woman aged about thirty. Seeing me frightened her, even if she made out she hadn't noticed me and merely quickened her pace a little. She wasn't far from her destination and she rushed into a building, after hurriedly keying in her entry code. I was relieved for her. Sometimes the people you meet are so tired they've lost all fear or curiosity. I'm not talking about the drug-addicts or the people who've drunk too much, though you can never be entirely sure of what you're seeing. They walk with a fixed stare, giving the impression they're at the end of their tether. You'd like to talk to them but you know it's impossible.

I think I have a bit of a temperature. I'll go and sleep in a hotel tonight, the more comfortable of the two. I wonder what the winter will be like and suddenly realize how madly I've been behaving. Where is all this taking me?

I note down these few words as I'm having a coffee at the Rendez-vous. Maria was in a sullen mood when I turned up and she pointed out that normally she doesn't serve breakfast. But I looked so weary that she gave in and went and bought a fresh baguette.

She sat at my table and watched me eat my bread and jam.

'Are you coming tomorrow evening? The artists will be here. There'll be quite an atmosphere. Your friend Dominique's coming.'

'I don't know.'

'Oh yes you do. I'm going to make rabbit stew.'

It pleased me that she talked about 'my friend' Dominique. That was balm for the soul, as the expression goes. My pained body definitely needs embalming, needs perfuming and swathing in bandages. All that's left of me is a sort of living corpse, a waking mummy. For a second I think of my Mercedes ambulance—ambulance or van—the Mercedes I'm hanging around in like a deadbeat who's on his very last legs or perhaps already   dead. By night in the *quinzième*, I'm just a stiff in a Mercedes.

'She asked about you yesterday. She really likes you. Dominique.'

'That's nice. Me too. I like her.'

Maria had assumed the air of a go-between. She was looking at me with a benevolent, collusive smile. That bucked me up. Her words had lent substance to a fleeting excitement that felt like a desire to live.

All the same, I really had a pain in my back.

July

In the end, the dinner at the Rendez-vous didn't go too badly. A soberer affair than last time. These artists are less bohemian than they try to make out. All they talked about this evening was their holiday plans. And *I*'m the civil servant! Dominique came and sat next to me. I wondered for a moment how she could be interested in me. Her interest is gratifying—why hide the fact?—but I'm at least twenty years older than she is and don't seem particularly youthful. She sees me write but she must surely have an idea that I'm not really a writer. If that were the case then, given my lifestyle, I'd be in the category of 'failed author' or 'literary outcast', to use a more elevated term. Yet I intrigue her, and this evening I found out why. She guessed I was more eccentric—or madder—than I'd wanted to let on. When we left the Rendez-vous, after giving Robert and Maria a goodnight hug, some of the party decided to go and have a last drink in Montparnasse. She said she'd rather go for a little walk, took me by the arm and dragged me off into the rue des Morillons. We walked a little way towards the parc Brassens. She stopped, looked me in the eye and asked me jokily, though a slight tremor in her voice made me feel she was afraid of touching on a taboo, of 'overstepping the mark', as the cliché-mongers put it: 'So are you going to show me your fine Mercedes?' I pretended not to understand and I wasn't, in fact, sure what she was getting at. I replied that it was an old car of no interest whatever but she drove home her point: 'Big enough for you to live in all the same!'

'I'm sorry,' she went on. 'The other night I was feeling down in the dumps in my room and went out to get some air. I was wandering round haphazardly and came to a street—I forget the name or, rather, I've never known its name—the one that runs alongside the tracks at Montparnasse station and, from a distance, I saw you get into your car. Since the car didn't start, I came closer and it didn't take long to see you were settling down for the night there. I didn't dare show myself.'

'It's the rue Fondary,' I said, for something to say.

'Is that right?'

She fell silent for a moment, a faint smile playing on her lips.

'Do you know, it's one of my longstanding fantasies to live in a car?'

We sat down at a cafe that was still open on the rue Brancion and she began to talk about herself. With one little secret leading to another, I joined in. Memories of childhood and adolescence first, especially holidays, since we were both city kids. We exchanged postcards, so to speak: my Brittany before she was born, her South of France at a point when my attention had already turned to taxpayers. We alluded to the different changes in our civil status: marriages followed by divorces, two to one in my favour. Then to our respective careers: hers has been more brilliant than mine but I made her laugh by assuring her that the job of tax inspector was mainly, in my view, a legal way of exploring society and individuals in depth—a bit like that of solicitor or barrister. A life, we soon agreed—though it was no great discovery—can be summed up in a few words. All in all, there isn't much to be said about it. What does take time, though, and here we were also in agreement, are the hesitations about the present and the near future, which are constantly, repeatedly up for discussion in one form or another.

She talked more than I did. I wanted to let her know that I'd too much of a sense of the ridiculous to try to 'court' her (even my vocabulary is dated). Out of frankness or shyness, I told her my age, adding that I was too aware of never having been able to control my past to aspire now to manage what came next. She pointed out that, if everything repeated itself, then we had as much experience at the age of forty as at sixty, which amounted to saying that experience served no purpose.

However, we clearly enjoyed exchanging these hard-bitten remarks. We ordered another drink. She liked the idea of my 'car-borne escape', as she put it. Personally, I was inclined to see it as a final running-aground after a life spent sailing round blindly. She took me to task over that: I was, in fact, a thwarted adventurer who'd finally found the courage—or the opportunity—to express himself, she said. She disclosed that she herself spent part of the year in a camper van, which made it easy for her to get to the places she liked to observe and depict: motorways, car parks, service stations, camp sites, the seaside—all those places where she felt more alone since everyone else went round in groups.

'The lorry drivers meet fellow drivers at all the parking areas: they recognize each other and chat together. In summer, the lovers are all on honeymoon; they're inseparable, ostentatiously joined at the hip, going about as couples even to buy chewing gum or fill up the car. As for the little "typically French" families, they act like flocks of penguins when they're on holiday, sticking tightly together in the queue for the toilets, for ice creams or the cash desk. The title of my next exhibition will be *The Happiness Factory* or something of that sort. It won't be ironic but ambiguous. I'm going to throw myself into it, as from next week.'

It was then we began sketching out some plans. I told her I'd really like to take a look at her work and I'd like to go down to the south too in the next few days. She laughed. 'Do you want to make a date to meet at a motorway services? Go on then, you're on!' She shot me a look of vaguely maternal benevolence, which took years off me.

At the end we were hardly saying anything. A gust of wind shook the trees in the park. She looked at her watch and gave a sigh. 'It's time for bed.' She put her hand on mine and, fairly briskly and with a cheery gleam in her eye, said: 'Come on, let's go to my place. We're not going to end the night on the back seat of a car.'

July

I got lost in the twelfth arrondissement. I'd taken the Métro out towards Daumesnil. Looking at the underground map in my diary, I'd realized there were station names out there, such as Michel-Bizot and Bel-Air, that didn't mean much to me. I got out somewhere or other—I forget just where—and, with a touch of boredom, a vague sadness generated not by melancholia but uninterest, became lost in a neighbourhood where nothing caught my eye, doubtless because I'd no memories of the place. After a whole series of twists and turns, I found myself back at la Porte Dorée. The foliage of the bois de Vincennes attracted me for a moment (when I was a child we sometimes went to watch the rowers on the lake or the apes in the zoo), but I was tired and flopped down on the terrace of a brasserie.

A shower forced me to retreat indoors. A number of sports fans were drawn to a tennis match being shown on television. From the wall seat I'd slumped into, I too looked up to follow the vicissitudes of the contest rather lazily. A great beanpole of a man came over, glass of white wine in hand, and drew me into conversation.

'He's good, that Federer, isn't he?'

'Very good,' I replied a bit feebly, making a thumbs-up gesture for youthful effect.

'I like tennis,' the beanpole went on. 'And all sports, in fact.'

'What do you play?' I asked, faking interest.

It would have been better to have said nothing. Encouraged by the interest I seemed to be showing, he asked if he could join me and set about analyzing the strengths and weaknesses of the world's top twenty tennis players. He'd played at a very high level, he confided, but he'd had to give it up because of all the plotting against him. 'And then my true vocation is the theatre,' he went on. 'I'm director of the twelfth-arrondissement drama school.' I admitted to being impressed. He conceded that, at twenty-four years of age, it really wasn't bad at all. He wasn't old but I had him down as older than twenty-four. 'I like La Fontaine,' he exclaimed suddenly and, putting on the requisite dramatic intonation, began to recite 'The Wolf and the Lamb', followed by 'The Cobbler and the Financier', all without pause. It was impressive. He offered to buy me dinner. I declined his offer and even refused to have another beer with him. I found his blue, transparent gaze troubling. He kept his eyes fixed on me all the while but, though he never averted his gaze, I had the impression he wasn't seeing me.

We exchanged a few more comments on the tennis match, which we continued to follow absentmindedly. Then he suddenly confided that what had given him a start in life was the literary success he'd experienced a few years earlier. 'Sales of two hundred thousand at the age of nineteen—that's not given to everyone,' he declared. At that same instant I spotted an anxious—and suddenly sharper—glance in my direction, as though he was afraid I wouldn't believe him.

I suddenly realized that he was mad and had once and for all crossed the invisible boundary-line that would eternally separate him from those he approached to accept his offer of a drink or dinner. Feeling both sympathy and fear, I got up, alleging a sudden desire to take a pee, and went downstairs to the toilet. When I came back up, I beckoned the waiter over, slipped him a ten-euro note and sidled away without further ado.

August

I turn up on time at the meeting place.

The Bois-au-Loup services are well designed for holidaymakers. There's a 'play area' outside the cafeteria with little slides, swings and even a sandpit, which must annoy those fathers who like to keep their cars clean. The cafeteria itself is charming. It's self-service but there are staff who clear and wipe the tables as soon as people leave. The whole place is 'well kept up', as they say. I got there around four o'clock in the afternoon and grabbed myself a 'Healthy Option' sandwich—lettuce, tomato, mayonnaise and slices of radish. Once I'd got the sandwich down me, I headed for the machine serving coffee and other hot drinks. I ordered an espresso, then went back to the till where all the last-minute impulse-buys are laid out. I bought myself a chocolate-coated energy bar and went back to the machine for another coffee.

I strolled round the shop for a little while. I looked over all the local produce—the red berry jams, the mountain honeys, the cellophane-wrapped cheeses, cellophane-wrapped local hams and cellophane-wrapped bilberry tarts. They also had a special offer on DVDs. There are certain objects I'm always drawn to in this kind of place, probably because, not having been a boy scout, I never went camping as a child and have always dreamt of doing so. I'm talking about pocket torches, multi-blade knives, sports watches that are 'waterproof to a depth of sixty feet' and the like, but I resisted the temptation to acquire any of these things. I was happy just to buy a newspaper and go and read it in the car. After half an hour, I got out to stretch my legs. I hesitated over buying a detective novel, but in the end decided to have a Coke instead as I took in a bit of the Olympic fencing in Beijing. The sound was off but there was such a buzz in the shop that you'd have thought you were at the venue. I came back out again. The lines of cars were lengthening round the petrol pumps. Mothers and children were leaving the queues to rush to the cafe or toilets. I went back across the car park, heading for the 'picnic area' that had been laid out on the side of a hill. It afforded quite a nice view of the surrounding slopes. There was a table free, one of those big tables that seem to have been carved straight out of some massive ancient oak with benches from the same tree. Actually, it wasn't very comfortable since, as soon as I shuffled up to stop myself falling over backwards, the tops of my thighs banged against the table. Either that or I've put on weight and a few inches. I eventually decided to sit astride the bench and started to do a crossword.

Dominique had warned me that, given the meandering route she was planning to take, she wasn't certain to be on time. By eight in the evening,

I had to accept she was going to be late. At nine I had steak and pan-fried potatoes in the cafeteria, then set about writing my diary.

August

She arrived at ten in the evening, confused and tear-
ful, explaining that she'd stayed longer than planned
at the filling station near Montluçon which she
intended to use as the centrepiece of her exhibition—'an enormous service station, a cathedral, a
monster of a place'—but that the main problem
was she'd had engine trouble as she was leaving the
place. 'Nothing serious, the ignition—spark plugs
sooted up, I think. But what a hassle to get someone
to take a look at it. You'd think the service station
were in cahoots with the towing people . . .'

We went to buy biscuits from the garage.
When we came back, she poured me a whisky. We
clinked glasses and she made her proposal:

'It's tomorrow you're supposed to be seeing
your friends?'

'Yes.'

'Listen, I know you've waited a long time for
me and I hate to say this, but I'm knackered. I feel
dirty, sweaty and horrible. I'd like our reunion to be
more elegant . . . nicer. Are you with me?'

'Absolutely.'

'Here's what I suggest. Let's try and each get a
few hours' sleep—separately. Tomorrow you go see
your friends while I go on with my work, first here,
then at another place, near Ussel. The day after

tomorrow, we can meet up at a lovely spot, a place you'll adore, the Auberge de la Truite d'Or near Bugeat, twenty miles or so past Meymac, on the banks of the Vézère. So you don't get the wrong idea, let me say it's a country inn I first got to know with my parents, two or three years ago.'

'That's an excellent suggestion,' I replied (and I was sincere; the Truite d'Or sounded more attractive than the Bois-au-Loup—and I hadn't formed any ideas, wrong or otherwise). 'But don't be surprised not to see me in the morning. I'm probably going to leave very early.'

So, in short, this new rendezvous replaced the old one. I was delighted with the idea. And she really was 'out on her feet'. I went off and fell fast asleep in the car but I woke again almost immediately. In fact, as soon as Dominique had said how tired she was and talked of the Truite d'Or, it had been in my mind to take off from there.

When I left the Bois-au-Loup services, it was around three o'clock. I wasn't sleepy any more. I wanted to drive. I went off down the motorway, past the exit I should have taken. That meant an extra thirty miles or so, sixty in all. With no one round, the night belonged to me. My full headlights carved distinct shapes out of the darkness, shapes demarcated by the central reservation, the yellow and white lines slipping by and the blue, brightly lettered signs that loomed up and just as suddenly disappeared, bearing the legend 'Tulle 40' or 'Brive-la-Gaillarde 66'. From time to time, when a distant halo of light indicated another traveller approaching in the opposite direction, I dipped my headlights, as though tipping him a knowing wink, and instantaneously the darkness came towards me. As I left the motorway, the sky growing dim overhead, I slipped incognito into deserted villages and skimmed by darkened areas of countryside without waking them, until at last I saw the first lights come on.

I was driving rather absent-mindedly, not very fast but absent-mindedly. At the end of a long, straight stretch of road that seemed to run right off into the forest ahead, I was caught out by a bend I hadn't seen coming. I braked violently. The car zigzagged, took a lump out of the verge and came to a halt beside a little rocky ravine.

It had all happened very quickly. I wiped the sweat from my face and got out without closing the door. I could feel my heart beating. I took a few steps in the silence of dawn, did a few stretching exercises, then got back behind the wheel and set off again, driving slowly. All was calm and peaceful once more. The engine ticked over noiselessly. My fear had gone and I was, in fact, starting to feel a kind of elation. I parked the car at the end of a path that ran off into the forest. I got out and followed it for a few dozen yards and sat down on a tree trunk by the entrance to a clearing made by the foresters. In a few hours the place would doubtless be overrun by lorries and mechanical saws. In the meantime, all I was aware of were the sighs of the forest, like a slow breathing. As day began to dawn, the wind was getting up.

My heart was gripped by the certainty I was at a turning point in my life—at *the* turning point in my life—and I don't know whether I was happy or in despair.

By good fortune I found a cafe open at Bourg-Saint-Jean, even though it wasn't yet seven, and I spent some time there writing up my diary.

Mid-August

I arrived around eleven in the morning. Andrée suggested that Albert and I should get out from under her feet while she prepared lunch. We took the path that runs from their house and snakes round the hill before dropping down into Saint-Marcellin. When I get back together with Albert, it's always the same. First we hug and compliment each other ('You're looking well . . .'), then we go straight on to some topical subject or an anecdote from our past, as though we were picking up a conversation we'd just broken off a few minutes earlier to go and answer the telephone or turn down the gas on the cooker.

When we got to the village, we sat ourselves down in the sun outside the Café de la Mairie. I was happy to rediscover the ordered calm of rural married life for which Albert had opted some years earlier and he was visibly happy to welcome me. He admitted that he felt the urge from time to time to pop back to Paris but he didn't have the heart. 'What would I do there? I don't know many people any more and I'm not big on memories.' I could understand him. I confided that I often felt the opposite urge, the desire to escape and bury myself in some rural haven, but that I didn't feel up to that either. 'Then come down to our place, to indulge your fantasies and to give us a bit of a break,' he said.

We set off back, slowly, since the return journey involved quite a stiff climb. It occurred to me to tell him I was trying to get back to writing and perhaps I'd let him see my scribblings some day. I could feel myself colouring up before I'd even opened my mouth. I wasn't afraid of his reactions, as he's so kind, but I couldn't bear to hear myself speak the words. I said nothing.

In the afternoon, Andrée decided we should take advantage of the good weather and go over to the lake for a bit of a swim. Albert's one indulgence is his little Italian convertible and we all three squeezed on to its front seat. It was a wild little episode. We sped along with the wind in our hair, though we never actually went above 40 mph. Albert reminded us that, some years ago, we'd seen *Butch Cassidy and the Sundance Kid* together. He pointed out that Andrée was still the spitting image of Katharine Ross and he left it to me to decide which of us looked more like Paul Newman than Robert Redford. We went back to the house for a drink before dinner. Albert was wonderfully relaxed, even if he did talk a bit too much about the past. But we're at an age when, among friends, we yield at times to that temptation. Evening in the garden was one of those rare moments whose intensity depends more on a sense of emptiness than over-fullness. Andrée, Albert and I together gave in to the mildness of the air, the taste of the white Burgundy and the brilliance of the sun dying on the horizon.

Mid-August

I met up with Dominique again at the inn. We took
an early dinner. The service was meticulous; they
were clearly trying to make their guests feel they
were at a high-class establishment. We must have
looked like a sensible, settled couple who had come
to celebrate an anniversary or rediscover a place
we'd frequented in the past. She was no more at
ease than I was in the role and we were short on
topics of conversation. In the bedroom, we leaned
for a moment on the sill of the window that looked
out over the river. She said the water was making
so much noise we'd have trouble getting to sleep.
However, she hadn't noticed the double glazing.
When we closed the window, we were surprised
how quiet it was. She said she needed to empty her
mind. I laid her on the bed, removed her skirt and
blouse, lay down beside her and took her hand. We
lay there a long time without sleeping, exchanging
a word from time to time before finally slipping into
sleep. At dawn, she wanted to make love to me but
I was exhausted and not feeling up to it. She fell
back asleep in my arms.

'Listen . . .'

She had slowly turned her head towards me as
it nestled comfortably in the pillow. She gazed deep
into the eyes I was forced to raise towards her from

the armchair which I'd pulled up beside the bed and curled up in.

'Did I tell you about the little house I have in the Touraine? I'm going to move in there for a while. I've got work to do. I have to prepare that exhibition I told you about. I've decisions to make, pictures to finish. An exhibition is a work in itself. I need time and quiet to get it all together. Why not come and live with me for a while? There's room. You could write if you like. It would be nice. I'd make log fires. We could chat. There's a man with a little vineyard next door and he brings me more wine than you'll ever be able to put away . . .'

She spoke faster and faster. She seemed to be doing so from shyness, and also because she realized she was suggesting that I change my life. She piled on the details. Nothing was left out: mushrooming in autumn, walks in the forest, the riverside, the chateaux of the Loire, but also the high-speed railway line nearby and Paris just a stone's throw away. She conjured up a series of images in me that gave rise in turn to a string of others—like a half-forgotten film I was seeing again.

But I wasn't at the cinema. It wasn't about re-living a piece of my past preserved on celluloid. It was about my life, real life, which only too often rehashes the same old things and goes round in circles. From the depths of my tiredness, I sensed the same distaste forming within me that had come,

several times, from a sense that my life was beginning to stutter and stammer and that, though I
thought I was starting something fresh, I was in fact
just repeating myself.

That absence that had hollowed out an unfath-
omable void over which I hovered each day, fighting
the sense of vertigo but constantly drawn towards
it—that feeling of absence I can't name, because
none of the words that suggest themselves (pain,
sorrow, regret, nostalgia, unhappiness) quite encap-
sulates it—was something I didn't want to give up.
It was the most authentic, most personal thing I
had. It was what made me 'me' and not someone
else. In a way, that very present absence helped me
to live—or, rather, to survive. It was no doubt des-
tined to disappear one day, to fade with time like
everything else, becoming an absence of absence, a
total emptiness, death. Or perhaps rebirth? I had
known those long night-time periods from which
you suddenly emerge without immediately realiz-
ing you've done so, those fresh dawns after a storm.
But there's a time for rebirths and a time for giving
up. Now, the simple sayings, the old saws and bits
of ready-made wisdom that annoyed me so much
when I was younger ('act your age,' 'if youth but
knew, if old age but could,' 'there's a time for everything') pressed themselves on me physically. The
memory of the woman who'd left me had faded
and its passing left me alone with myself. All that
remained was to face up squarely, without evasion

or illusion, to the final reckoning—that reckoning which deprived even the word 'loneliness' of all meaning. The time for stopping by the roadside was past. For the first time in my life I resisted the illusion of beginning again.

As though reading my mind and in a voice already betraying a hint of resignation, she tried to tell me that she was starting to understand what made me tick, that I needed, above all, to arrive and to leave, to leave and to arrive, to pass through. In spite of the camper van (which was, after all, just a house she carried round with her), she liked to wait and have others come to her. She liked arrivals and she could cope with departures. So, that fitted together nicely, didn't it? Then, doubtless to head off any discussion, she quickly added that she'd go on her way that very evening, head back towards the Loire and use the trip to take a few last photos.

I knelt beside the bed and leaned my head on it. She ruffled my hair almost absent-mindedly and whispered, 'You can come and see me whenever you like, Mr Tax Inspector.'

'I certainly will,' I replied.

I went back to Andrée and Albert's. I'd promised them I would. A last silent, tranquil day, a day as fragile as a brightening of the weather at evening's end. I didn't have the heart to talk, to tell them how things were. They wouldn't have understood me. They couldn't even imagine what was happening to me. After a few hours, once the initial emotion had passed, I felt even lonelier with them than I did on the streets of Paris. Out of place. That was it: I felt out of place, literally and irremediably out of place.

It's difficult to play a role when there are no grounds for that role any more, difficult to stay in your place when you've lost that place or to exist in another person's dwelling when you yourself have no fixed abode, are without hearth or home, are almost nameless.

When I came off the Paris ring road at porte de la Plaine, I had the weird sensation of plunging simultaneously into different periods of my life. Over the years, I'd often come back to Paris by this route, which took me straight back to the flat. I'd got into the habit of it. I came home without giving it a thought.

Weakly, I felt the need to run the full gamut of sensations straight away. I picked up some washing I'd forgotten at the launderette and went to the baker's to buy a croissant, popping my head round the butcher's door on the way. I was a bit disappointed. My presence seemed so normal that, once I'd been through the ritual of initial questions, they hardly paid me any mind. I did appreciate them asking if my holidays had gone well, all the same, and adding once or twice, mechanically, 'It's nice to be home again, isn't it?' I went so far as to knock on the door of the caretaker at my old block to ask her if there had been any mail but her office was closed up.

I went straight to the Rendez-vous des Amis. Robert and Maria were up to their eyeballs that evening. There was a big crowd in. 'And then we're closing tomorrow for three weeks,' Maria confided, as if to excuse the general air of feverishness, as she brought me a *crème brûlée* I hadn't ordered. All the same, she stopped at the next table to discuss the day's big news. That morning, coming back from the wholesale market at Rungis, Robert had noticed that the body of François, the beggar with the gentle eyes and the furry toy dog, was stretched out on the pavement opposite in a weird position. It took him all of a minute to realize he wasn't asleep and to phone the emergency services.

I went back slowly to my car and sat down at the wheel. I sat there motionless for a long time. I was thinking back over the hours spent driving after I'd left the Bois-au-Loup services, of the moment I'd nearly gone off the road and the minutes of calm that had followed. I told myself it was time to stop lying to myself the way I lied to other people. It was time to give up the pretences, the vague literary aspirations and my little act in the fifteenth arrondissement. It was time for a change of scenery. I decided to 'do a moonlight flit' without saying goodbye to anyone and I set off driving slowly towards the Seine.